Learning to read. Reading to learn!

LEVEL ONE Sounding It Out Preschool–Kindergarten
For kids who know their alphabet and are starting to sound out words.

learning sight words • beginning reading • sounding out words

LEVEL TWO Reading with Help Preschool–Grade 1
For kids who know sight words and are learning to sound out new words.

expanding vocabulary • building confidence • sounding out bigger words

LEVEL THREE Independent Reading Grades 1–3
For kids who are beginning to read on their own.

introducing paragraphs • challenging vocabulary • reading for comprehension

LEVEL FOUR Chapters Grades 2–4
For confident readers who enjoy a mixture of images and story.

reading for learning • more complex content • feeding curiosity

Ripley Readers Designed to help kids build their reading skills and confidence at any level, this program offers a variety of fun, entertaining, and unbelievable topics to interest even the most reluctant readers. With stories and information that will spark their curiosity, each book will motivate them to start and keep reading.

PUBLISHING

Vice President, Licensing & Publishing Amanda Joiner
Editorial Manager Carrie Bolin

Editor Jordie R. Orlando
Writer Korynn Wible-Freels
Designer Scott Swanson
Reprographics Bob Prohaska
Production Design Luis Fuentes

Published by Ripley Publishing 2021

10 9 8 7 6 5 4 3 2 1

Copyright © 2021 Ripley Publishing

ISBN: 978-1-60991-440-0

For more information regarding permission, contact:
VP Licensing & Publishing
Ripley Entertainment Inc.
7576 Kingspointe Parkway, Suite 188
Orlando, Florida 32819

Email: publishing@ripleys.com
www.ripleys.com/books
Manufactured in China in May 2020.

First Printing

Library of Congress Control Number:
2020937133

PUBLISHER'S NOTE
While every effort has been made to verify the accuracy of the entries in this book, the Publisher cannot be held responsible for any errors contained in the work. They would be glad to receive any information from readers.

PHOTO CREDITS

Cover (background) © LIUSHENGFILM/Shutterstock **3** (background) © LIUSHENGFILM/Shutterstock **4-5** © Mazur Travel/Shutterstock **8-9** © AaronTsui/Shutterstock **10-11** Mark Edward Smith/Solent News/Shutterstock **16-17** Todd Lewis/Barcroft Cars/Barcroft Media via Getty Images **18-19** WENN **22-23** Caters News **24-25** Tony Kyriacou/Shutterstock **26-27** ALEXANDER NEMENOV/AFP via Getty Images **Master Graphics** Created by Scott Swanson

All other photos are from Ripley Entertainment Inc. Every attempt has been made to acknowledge correctly and contact copyright holders and we apologize in advance for any unintentional errors or omissions, which will be corrected in future editions.ground

Ripley Readers

Crazy Cars!

All true and unbelievable!

Ripley
PUBLISHING

a Jim Pattison Company

Come and see these neat rides!

This car is
so little!

Only one person
can fit in it!

Did you see that car go by?

It is the fastest one in the world!

Look! That car can go in the water!

Do you want to take a ride in this shoe?

It must have taken a long time to make a car from matchsticks!

A car that looks like food!

Do you like bananas?

Have you seen this fish car
that plays music?

How funny!

Wow! That car is so pretty!

Blast off!

Do not stand too close
to this truck!

It took twelve miles of red yarn
to make this ride!

Do you play with LEGO?

Have you made something this big?

Boo! This white coffin car is cool *and* creepy!

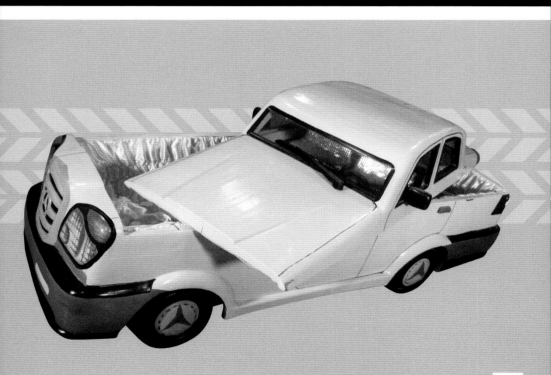

Bumpers are not only for cars!

Can you think up a new ride?

LEVEL ONE · Sounding it out

RIPLEY Readers

All true and unbelievable!

Ready for More?

Ripley Readers feature unbelievable but true facts and stories!

 LEVEL ONE · Sounding it out

 LEVEL TWO · Reading with help

 LEVEL THREE · Independent reading

 LEVEL FOUR · Chapters

 **Bears!**

 **Caves!**

 **Animal Imposters!**

 **Take Flight!**

 **Sports!**

 **Raging Raptors!**

 **Odd Ocean!**

 **Mythical Creatures!**

For more information about
Ripley's Believe It or Not!, go to www.ripleys.com